Jared and His Brother

written by Tiffany Thomas
illustrated by Nikki Casassa

CFI · An imprint of Cedar Fort, Inc. · Springville, Utah

HARD WORDS:
Babel, Heaven, speech, talk

PARENT TIP: The illustrations on each page will help your child understand and learn the words.

This is Jared
and his brother.
They are
men of God.

The people in
Babel are bad.

3

The people want to go to heaven.

They do not want to repent.

The people try to build a
tower to go to heaven.

God is sad
and mad at
the people.

God changes how the people talk.

Jared's brother is sad.
He prays to God.

God does not change
his family's speech.

Jared and his brother leave
Babel with their families.

They go to the sea.

The end.

ISBN 13: 978-1-4621-4337-5

Published by CFI, an imprint of Cedar Fort, Inc. • 2373 W. 700 S., Suite 100, Springville, UT 84663
Distributed by Cedar Fort, Inc., www.cedarfort.com

Cover design and interior layout design by Shawnda T. Craig
Cover design © 2022 Cedar Fort, Inc.
Printed in China • Printed on acid-free paper
10 9 8 7 6 5 4 3 2 1